Triple Crown

annotated by the author

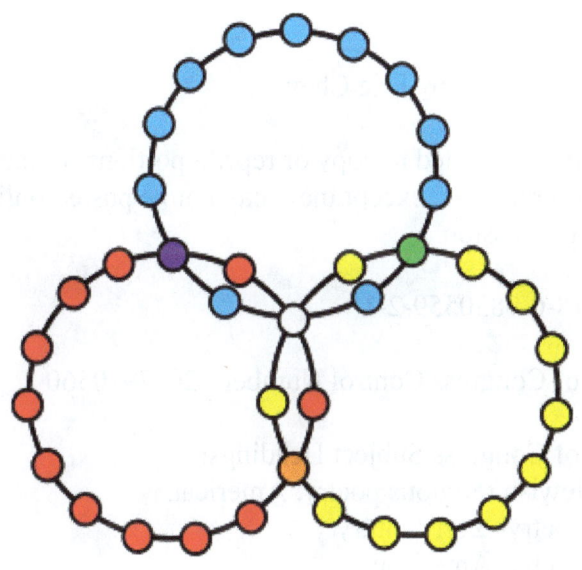

Eric Chevlen

Borromean Books
Youngstown, Ohio

Triple Crown

Copyright © 2017 by Eric Chevlen

Permission is granted to copy or reprint portions for any noncommercial use, except they may not be posted online without permission.

ISBN 978-0-9830559-2-1

Library of Congress Control Number: 2017910560

Library of Congress Subject Headings:
    Jewish religious poetry, American
    Poetry--21st century
    Poetry, American
    Religion and poetry
    Religious poetry, American
    Sonnets, American

Language is the gift God gave to man.
We, in turn, write poetry, who can.

Introduction

Triple Crown is, to my knowledge, the only triple heroic crown of sonnets in the English language. I believe it is the only such poetic work in any language. Therefore, some words of introduction are certainly appropriate, probably helpful, and possibly necessary.[1]

A crown of sonnets is a series of sonnets linked one to another, such that the last line of one poem is repeated as the first line of the subsequent poem. This process continues until the loop is closed by the last line of the last poem's being repeated as the first line of the first poem. A classic example of this is the exquisite seven poem crown of sonnets by John Donne entitled, aptly enough, *La Corona.*

A heroic crown of sonnets is a sonnet crown consisting of fourteen poems linked as described above. The added feature which makes the heroic crown more than simply a longer collection of poems is that the linking (repeated) lines of poetry themselves comprise another sonnet. Thus, a fifteenth sonnet is implicit in the fourteen sonnets explicitly stated in the heroic crown. This fifteenth sonnet is called the magistral sonnet. As an added feature, the magistral sonnet is often an acrostic, with the acronym embedded within it pithily summarizing the theme of the entire set.

One can represent a heroic crown of sonnets, then, as a series of small filled circles linked together into a larger circle, something like beads on a necklace. It will be readily apparent that one could have three such circles, with each circle

---

[1] The adverbs here decrease in intensity as the adjectives increase in intensity. A similar pattern is seen in Psalms 1:1. "The praises of Man are that he did not walk in the counsel of the wicked, nor stand in the path of the sinful, nor sit in the session of scorners." Walking by gives less exposure than standing, and standing gives less exposure than sitting. The wicked are worse than the sinful, and the sinful are worse than the scorners.

Triple Crown

intersecting the others at two places each. One of the sites of intersection is common to all three circles. (See figure below.) Each cycle of poetry, therefore, will contain three poems whose first lines also serve as first lines in poems of the other two cycles. This is the fundamental structure of *Triple Crown*.

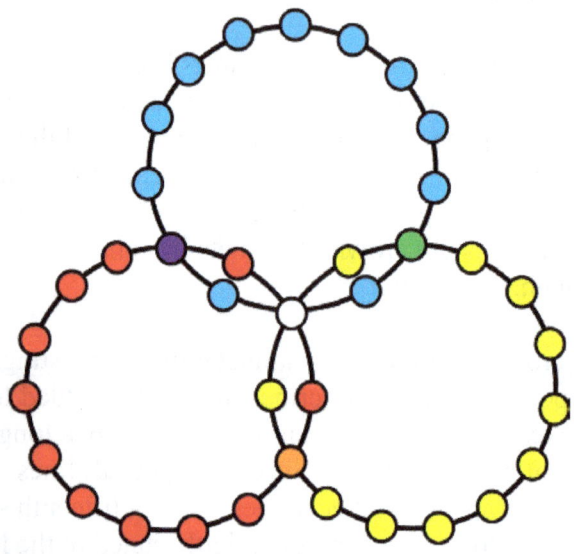

Triple Crown contains several other structural features. Naturally, the magistral sonnet of each cycle still serves as an acrostic. Additionally, the eighth line of each of the poems (excluding the magistral sonnets) also form an acrostic spanning the entire poetic work. In the text, the first letter of these lines is in bold font.

The three cycles of *Triple Crown* are not merely structured thematically; they are also structured chromatically. Indeed, the chromatic structure reflects the thematic structure.

Blue is the color ascribed to heaven and all that emanates from it. The magistral sonnet of the blue cycle is a recapitulation of the story of Creation, just as the poems within that cycle tell

Introduction

that story in greater detail. Every poem of the blue cycle, except as noted below, refers to some blue aspect of Creation.

Red represents conflict. The red cycle tells the stories of conflict in the lives of the three great kings of Israel—Saul, David, and Solomon. The magistral sonnet of that collection retells the story found in *Song of Songs*; that great poem, too, tells of the conflict—love, estrangement, and reconciliation—of God and the Jewish people. The poems of the red cycle, again with the exception noted below, reveal the redness of their subject.

Yellow is the color of dust, decline, and decay. The magistral sonnet of the yellow cycle summarizes the story of Job, and the poems of that cycle tell Job's story in greater detail. These poems, like those of the other two cycles, reflect their thematic color, except as noted below.

The exception to the color coding of each cycle is the result of the cycles intersecting. Where the blue and red cycles intersect, the thematic color must be purple. Where the blue and yellow cycles intersect, the thematic color must be green, and of course the intersection of the red and yellow cycles is portrayed, however implicitly, by the color orange. Where all three cycles intersect, the colors combine to make white light. The poems at that unique intersection are not sonnets, but villanelles.

Creation is known from afar. The blue cycle portraying Creation is therefore written primarily in the third person. Conflict is dyadic. The red cycle, therefore, is excerpts of dialogue, written primarily in the second person. Suffering is personal. The yellow cycle is written in the first person. There are, of course, other structural and thematic features in *Triple Crown*. I leave it to the reader to find or invent these, and to enjoy them.

Triple Crown

Opposite each poem in the book is a diagram indicating where, in the total structure, the poem lies. This should help keep the reader apprised as to his location within the entire work.

Triple Crown is not a collection of poems. It is a unified work, intended to be read in the order presented.

Introduction

Triple Crown

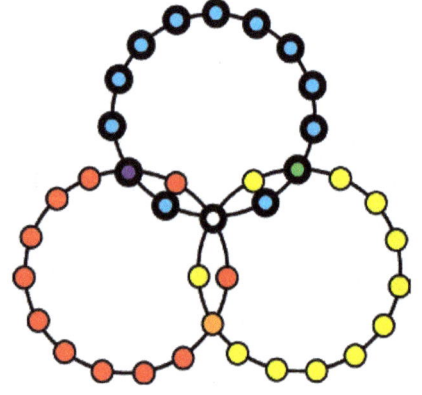

God's Blue Throne

Grandiloquent, creating with just speech,
O God, whom angels praise by day and night,
Deign these crowns, too, be worthy in Your sight.
Safeguard them nigh, and me, within Your reach.
Before the force of nature was unleashed,
"**L**et there be light," He said, and there was light.
(**U**p to us, the sparks to reunite.)
Evoked by love, the waves caress the beach.
The land is blanketed with grass and trees.
He fills the azure seas with teeming life,
Roaring beasts on land, with speech unblessed.
Over all His creatures, land and seas,
Nature's lord He sets, the man and wife.
Evermore and more, God grants us rest.

Triple Crown

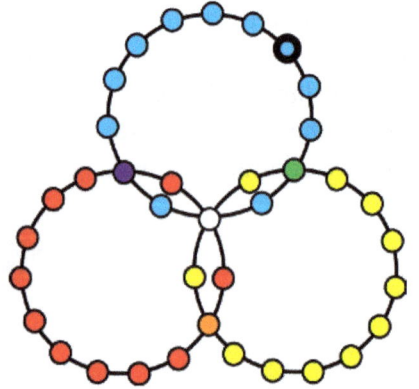

God's Blue Throne

Grandiloquent, creating with just speech,[1]
The echo of His first substantial[2] word,
Extending from creation's farthest reach
Suffuses our blue world, and still is heard.[3]
Its symmetry, established from the first,
Gives witness to inflation's breathless run,[4]
When all that is, or ever will be, burst,
When all the universe, like God, was one.
But now the echoes' waves are nearly still,
Perhaps would be the absolute of cold,[5]
If God did not observe them by His will,[6]
And constantly rejuvenate the old.
We too exist, Lord, only in Your sight,
O God, whom angels praise by day and night,

---

[1] See *Pirkei Avot* 5:1. "The world was created with ten utterances."
[2] The first words—"Let there be light"—created substance.
[3] The background cosmic radiation is the observable remnant of the Big Bang.
[4] The observable universe is remarkably uniform on a large scale. Since distant parts of the universe cannot communicate within the time since the Big Bang, this uniformity is evidence that the universe expanded explosively in an inflationary period shortly after the Big Bang.
[5] The temperature of the cosmic microwave background radiation is less than three degrees Celsius above absolute zero.
[6] One of the tenets of quantum mechanics is that a quantum level event transitions from potential to actual only upon observation.

Triple Crown

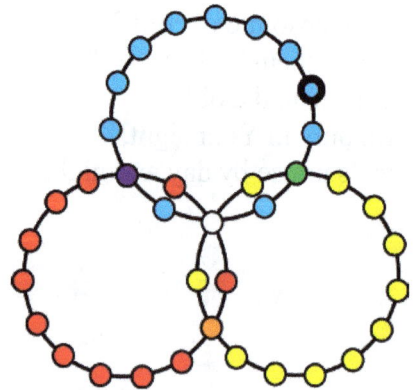

God's Blue Throne

O God, whom angels praise by day and night,[1]
A poor *paytan*[2] approaches Your blue throne[3]
To offer up before Your grandeur's height
These woven words,[4] these words of worth unknown.
O King, who was, who is, who e'er will be,
You gave three crowns,[5] a gift forevermore:
First priesthood's crown to Aaron's progeny,
In purity, forgiveness to implore,
Then crown of Torah gave to rectify
Your people, and the nations if they heed.
Though now in dust the kingship crown may lie
It yet will gleam on David and his seed.
Now humbly I Your lofty gifts requite;
Deign these crowns, too, be worthy in Your sight.

---

[1] See Babylonian Talmud (hereinafter referred to as Talmud Bavli) *Chullin* 91b. "And the angels do not sing above until Israel speaks below." Also see Isaiah 6:3 "And one [seraph] would call to another and say, 'Holy, holy, holy is the Lord of Hosts; the whole world is filled with His glory.'" Also see Deuteronomy 6:7. "…you shall speak of them…when you lie down and when you rise up."
[2] A *paytan* is a person who writes *piyyutim* (singular, *piyyut*). A *piyyut* is a Jewish liturgical poem, often based on a poetic scheme such as an acrostic.
[3] See Ezekiel 1:26. "Above the expanse that was over their heads was the appearance of sapphire stone in the likeness of a throne…"
[4] This is an *homage* to *'Anim Zemirot*, a *piyyut* attributed to the 12th century *paytan* Rav Yehudah HaChassid. Its opening lines are "I shall compose pleasant psalms, and weave together hymns."
[5] See *Pirkei Avot* 4:17. "Rabbi Shimon said, 'There are three crowns—the crown of Torah, the crown of priesthood, and the crown of kingship…'"

Triple Crown

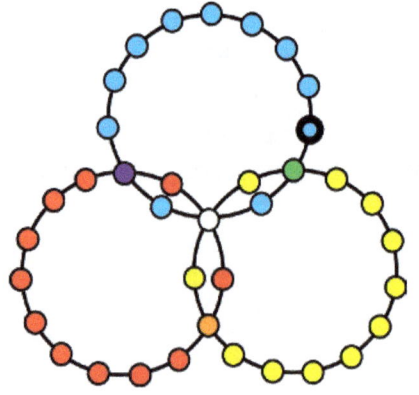

God's Blue Throne

Deign these crowns,[1] too, be worthy in Your sight,
These little crowns of ringlets yet unshorn,[2]
The foolishness of age,[3] and its delight,[4]
The love of children's children yet unborn.
They too may weave their crowns of praise in verse,
Amid life's multiplicity know One...[5]
Or—O forbid!—soul-sicken, hate and curse
The day that first was heard "Behold: a son!"[6]
Each generation weaves its crown anew.
Each generation adds its twisted thread,
Or sets upon the crown a jewel of blue
Amid the strands of gold and brass and lead.
Inured to the despair that life would teach,
Safeguard them nigh, and me, within Your reach.

---

[1] This is an *homage* to John Donne's sonnet crown *La Corona*. Its opening line is "Deign at my hands this crown of prayer and praise..."
[2] Among Chassidim it is customary not to cut a boy's hair until he is three years old. The first haircut is given religious significance in a ceremony called *upsharnish*.
[3] Grandparents lose their decorum around their young grandchildren.
[4] See Proverbs 17:6. "The crown of elders is grandchildren, and the glory of children is their parents."
[5] See Zechariah 14:9. "The Lord will be King over all the land; on that day the Lord will be One and His name will be One."
[6] See Genesis 29:32. "Leah conceived and bore a son, and she called his name Reuben, as she had declared, 'Because the Lord has discerned my humiliation, for now my husband will love me.'" "Reuben" in Hebrew means "see: a son!"

Triple Crown

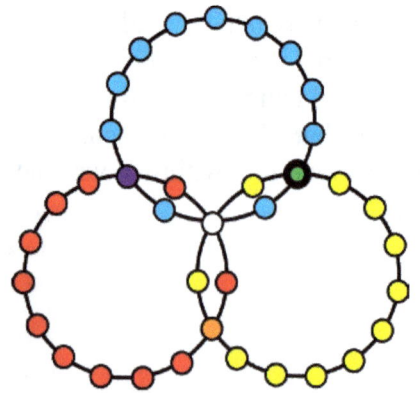

God's Blue Throne

Safeguard them nigh, and me, within Your reach.
Safeguard these sparks primaeval, holy sparks[1]
Suffusing all the world, a world in each,
All top and bottom strange and charming quarks.[2]
Safeguard the scintillation tinted green
Which spans between creation and the pit.[3]
Safeguard the holy glue[4] that binds unseen
Hadrons,[5] heaven—songs done[6] and songs unwrit.
Safeguard us too as we fulfill the task
To elevate the sparks from matter coarse,
To blow on glowing embers, and to bask
In light reborn returning to its source.
Safeguard us. We repair a wall first breached[7]
Before the force of nature was unleashed.

---

[1] It is a basic tenet of Lurianic Kabbalah that in the pre-temporal era of creation, God sent forth ten vessels of holy light, but the vessels shattered, scattering their sparks throughout the mundane world. The Ari (Rabbi Isaac Luria, 1534-1572) taught: "There is no sphere of existence, including organic and inorganic nature, that is not full of holy sparks which are mixed in with the *kelippot* [husks], and need to be separated from them and lifted up."

[2] Quarks are elementary particles which are fundamental constituents of matter. There are six types of quarks, known as flavors: up, down, strange, charm, top, and bottom.

[3] The green Earth exists as a temporal and spatial oasis between Creation and the final collapse of the solar system.

[4] Quarks are bound together by elementary particles called gluons to form neutrons or protons.

[5] Hadrons are elementary particles comprised of quarks +/- other elementary particles.

[6] An *homage* to the poetry of John Donne.

[7] See Isaiah 58:12. "Ancient ruins will be rebuilt through you, and you will restore generations-old foundations; and they will call you 'repairer of the breach' and 'restorer of paths for habitation.'"

Triple Crown

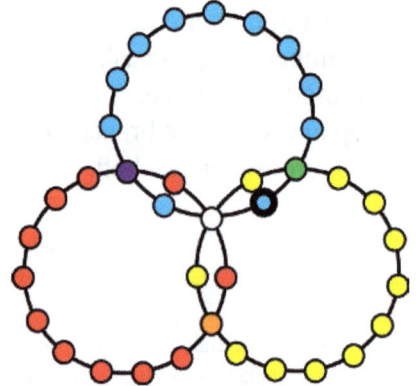

God's Blue Throne

Before the force of nature was unleashed
By Him whose nature knows of no before,[1]
He knew creation's purpose,[2] not yet reached,
A premonition then and evermore:
The sabbath rest, a foretaste of rebirth.[3]
He shaped the male and female and their need,
The animals and plants. He made the earth
In plenitude, for sustenance and seed.
The sun and moon and stars He made from naught,
And supernovae's ancient brilliant blast,
That heavy elements might there be wrought.[4]
Timeless, He is and sees the first and last:
That two small flames of blue she might ignite,[5]
"Let there be light," He said—and there was light.

---

[1] See Isaiah 44:6. "Thus said the Lord, King of Israel and its Redeemer, the Lord of Hosts: I am the first and I am the last, and aside from Me there is no God."

[2] See Genesis 2:3. "God blessed the seventh day and sanctified it, because on it He abstained from all His work which God created to make." The Sabbath is the culmination of Creation, the only day which God both blessed and sanctified.

[3] See Talmud Bavli *Berachos* 57b, which cites the Sabbath as a semblance of the world to come.

[4] After the Big Bang, the material universe was hydrogen and helium. Heavier elements were subsequently created in the collapse of stars, which we perceive as supernovae.

[5] The two small flames are the Sabbath candles.

Triple Crown

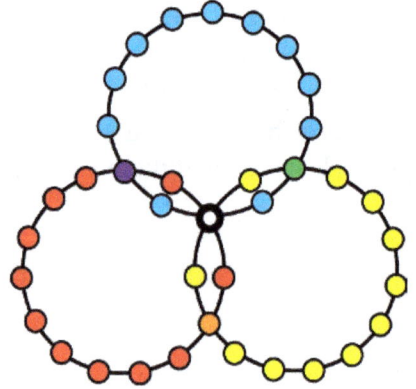

God's Blue Throne

"Let there be light," He said, and there was light.[1]
The scattered sparks flew each its willful way.
(Up to us, the sparks to reunite.)

And there was evening, darkness renamed night,[2]
And there was morning on that unique day[3]
"Let there be light," He said, and there was light.

The spheres that held them shattered. Sparks in flight
Now fled in hell-bent scattered disarray.
(Up to us, the sparks to reunite.)

How glorious stretched eternity, and bright.
How pure and perfect past and future lay.
"Let there be light," He said, and there was light.

But pure and perfect bore within it blight;
Eternity proved mother to decay.
(Up to us, the sparks to reunite.)

Or is this greater glory, recondite,
A co-creating part for us to play?
"Let there be light," He said, and there was light.
(Up to us, the sparks to reunite.)

---

[1] See Genesis 1:3. "God said, 'Let there be light,' and there was light."
[2] See Genesis 1:5. "God called the light 'day,' and the darkness He called 'night.'" Darkness existed before God named it "night."
[3] *Ibid.* "And there was evening and there was morning, one day." The evening and morning were called "one day," not a "first day." Until the creation of other days, there was no series of days of which one could be called the first.

Triple Crown

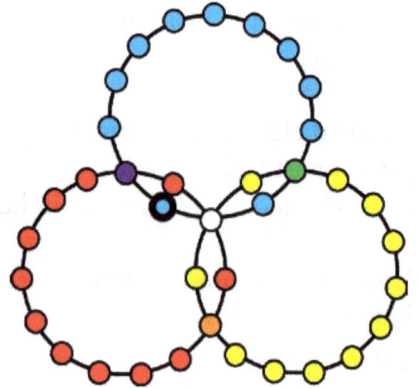

God's Blue Throne

Up to us, the sparks to reunite
Into a realm of holiness on earth;
To raise, redeem, the scattered shards of light
Inherent, hidden in apparent dearth;
To gather them and us upon a shore
Whose edge of blue abuts a sunless sea;[1]
And send them soaring homeward; to restore
To each the place where it was meant to be.
Each particle of light, a wave is too,[2]
And interferes with others in its course.[3]
To whom send such a message? Replies who?
Detected and reflected by what force?
And yet—like angels calling each to each,[4]
Evoked by love, the waves caress the beach.[5]

---

[1] Earth is a mostly blue sphere surrounded by a vast expanse of empty space.
[2] A fundamental principle of quantum mechanics is that a photon behaves like a particle or a like a wave, depending on how it is observed.
[3] The interference of light waves can encode information, as in holography.
[4] See Isaiah 6:3. "And one [seraph] would call to another and say, 'Holy, holy, holy is the Lord of Hosts; the whole world is filled with His glory.'"
[5] The divine reply reaches the interface of life and lifeless space.

Triple Crown

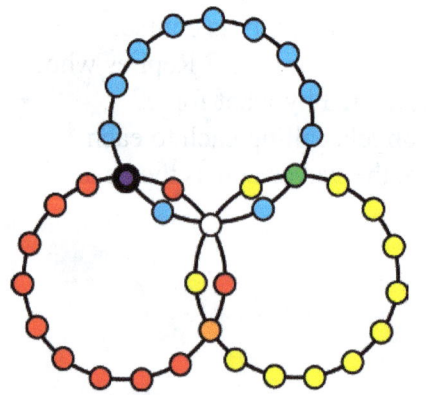

God's Blue Throne

Evoked by love, the waves caress the beach.[1]
The beach, in turn, yields grain by grain her sand,
Like lovers wrapped in rapture, each in each:
The ageless love of water and of land.
In tidal pools, in basins, in the muds
Of swamps and marshes, prairies soaked with rain,
In gullies gouged by angry ancient floods,
Here life may start, and end, and start again.[2]
Beneath the frost-tipped lilacs, earth is rife
With musty germinations. The untold
And ceaseless, restless writhing of new life
That stirs amid the rank decay of old
Lies hidden, fecundation no one sees:[3]
The land is blanketed with grass and trees.

---

[1] See Genesis 1:9. "God said, 'Let the waters beneath the heaven be gathered into one area, and let the dry land appear.' And it was so." Thus, the dry land appeared as a result of the gathering together of the waters of the sea, thereby also creating waves on the shores of the emerging dry land.
[2] Biologists believe that terrestrial life evolved from sea creatures in littoral zones.
[3] Human fecundation too lies hidden under blankets.

Triple Crown

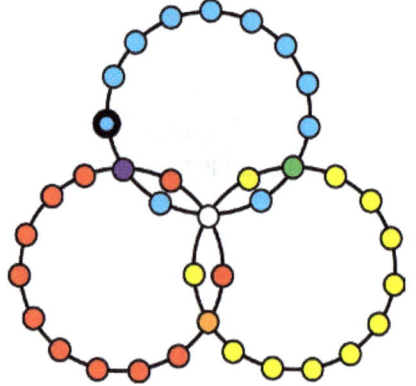

God's Blue Throne

The land is blanketed with grass and trees
But briefly. Then within its shroud of snow
It lies entombed in ice amid the freeze,[1]
Inert, dim light above, and none below.
Its lifeless monuments, the craggy heights,
Hold sway above the silent ice-draped plains,
While fossils of forgotten trilobites
Erode into unnumbered limestone grains
And blow to sea. But ah! the sea, the sea!
The sea has ever lived, has never ceased.
Its plankton exhale life at God's decree;[2]
Its depths provide our food and promised feast.[3]
God makes the sea abundant, vital, rife;
He fills the azure seas with teeming life.

---

[1] This poem describes the Ice Age.
[2] Half of atmospheric oxygen comes from plankton.
[3] See Talmud Bavli *Bava Basra* 75a. "The Holy One, blessed is He, will one day make a meal for the righteous from the flesh of the Leviathan."

Triple Crown

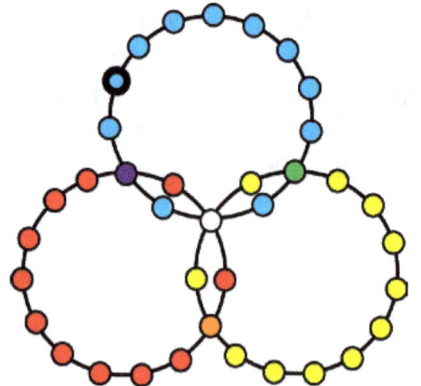

God's Blue Throne

He fills the azure seas with teeming life
But not His image.[1] That He would not keep
Amid the turbulence and tide, the strife
Of predator and prey within the deep.
Nor did He place His likeness in the breeze
Which blows alike for dust and cloud and hawk,
Indifferent, sowing pollen and disease.
He chose the land—is He not called the Rock?—[2]
To bear His image, soil of every clime,[3]
And formed the creature there upon the block
Where He will set His house again in time.[4]
He gave him speech. His creature-child can talk
And pray, and curse. Not so the rest:
Roaring beasts on land, with speech unblessed.

---

[1] Since God's image is a spiritual quality, not a physical appearance, it could have been granted to a creature of the sea or sky.

[2] See Psalms 18:3. "The Lord is my Rock, my Fortress, and my Rescuer…"

[3] See Rashi on Genesis 2:7. "God collected man's soil from all the earth, from the four directions, so that anywhere man may die, there the earth will take him in for burial."

[4] Adam was created at the site where the Temple would be built. See Maimonides, *Mishneh Torah, Hilchos Bais HaBechirah*, 2:2. "Adam, the first man, offered a sacrifice there and was created at that very spot, as our Sages said, 'Man was created from the place where he would find atonement.'" See also Jerusalem Talmud, *Nazir* 7:2. "The Holy One, Blessed be He, took a spoonful of dirt from the place of the altar, and with it created the first man. He said, 'May he be created from the altar, and so endure.'"

Triple Crown

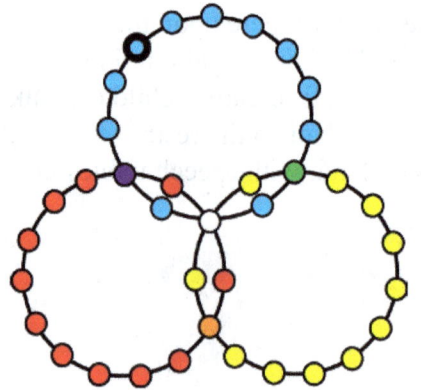

God's Blue Throne

Roaring beasts on land, with speech unblessed,
Exemplify in awe their Maker's might,
While humble creatures likewise manifest
The attributes that honor the upright.[1]
In modesty the cat heeds nature's call.
The ant will not purloin his fellow's grain.
In chastity the dove instructs us all
In how to mate for life, and so remain.
The rooster, in his wooing of the hen,
Reveals the innate wisdom that he knows—
Within a turquoise palace or a pen—
That every cock should coo before he crows.
God's providence extends, like His decrees,
Over all His creatures, land and seas.

---

[1] See Talmud Bavli *Eruvin* 100b. "Had not the Torah been given, we would have learned modesty from a cat, not to commit theft from an ant, not to commit adultery from a dove, and the proper manner of conduct for marital relations from a rooster, which first appeases its mate and then has relations with it."

Triple Crown

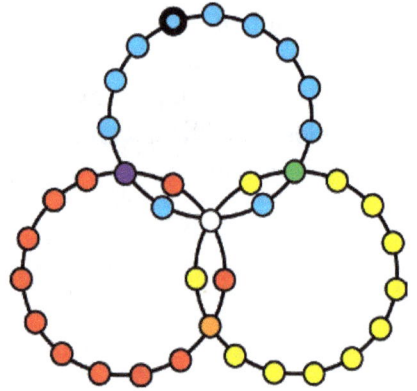

God's Blue Throne

Over all His creatures, land and seas,
A pair and paradox He sets to reign,
The creatures who reach higher on their knees,[1]
Whose aggrandizement ever is in vain.[2]
To know of good and evil and its tree,
They eat its fruit, and open wide their eyes,[3]
No longer good, no longer evil see
Discrete, but good-and-evil in disguise.[4]
A paragon[5] and paradox is man,
Alone allowed approach to God's blue throne,
Alone enabled to defy His plan,
Alone a soul interred in flesh and bone.
One soul placed in two bodies for their life,[6]
Nature's lord, He sets the man and wife.

---

[1] The Hebrew word for blessing, *berachah*, is etymologically related to the Hebrew word for knee, *barach*.
[2] See Genesis 11:4-9 concerning the Tower of Babel. "And they said, 'Come, let us build us a city, and a tower with its top in the heavens, and let us make a name for ourselves...'...And the Lord dispersed them from there over the face of the whole earth; and they stopped building the city."
[3] See Genesis 3:7. "Then the eyes of both of them were opened and they realized that they were naked..."
[4] The expression "good and evil" is a merism. Before the First Sin, Adam and Eve could easily distinguish between good and evil. After it, they saw deeds as a mixture of the two.
[5] See *Hamlet*, Act II Scene 2. "The paragon of animals!"
[6] See Zohar III, 7b. "The union of male and female is termed 'one.' ... For a male without a female is called 'half a body,' and a half is not 'one.' When the two halves unite, they then become one body, and they are then called 'one.'" See also Diogenes Laërtius, *Lives and Opinions of Eminent Philosophers*. "When asked what a friend (φίλος) is, [Aristotle] said, 'A single soul inhabiting two bodies.'"

Triple Crown

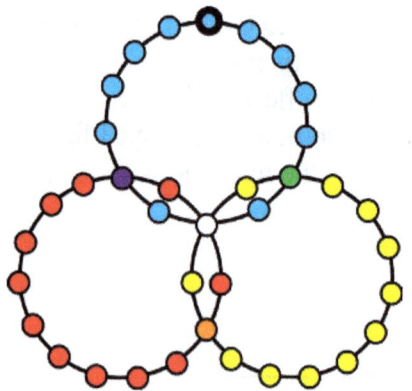

God's Blue Throne

Nature's lord He sets, the man and wife,
Into a paradise of their demesne,
But disobedience[1] and causeless strife[2]
Expel them to the thrall of death and pain,[3]
She, to bear her cyanotic young,
In clutch-throat anguish whisper, "Breathe, my child!"
And he, amid the brow-sweat, mud, and dung,
Dethroned as Eden's king, to tame the wild.
And yet...the source of blessings nonetheless
Ordains a day when tribulations end,
A day that man or God or both may bless,
And spirit over matter yet transcend:
No more weak days[4] in grubbing futile quest;
Evermore and more, God grants us rest.

---

[1] An *homage* to the first line of Milton's *Paradise Lost*.
[2] See Talmud Bavli *Yoma* 9b. "The Second Temple...was destroyed because of the gratuitous hatred that existed there."
[3] See Genesis 3:16-19. "I will greatly increase your suffering...through suffering shall you eat...for you are dust, and to dust shall you return."
[4] "Weak days" is a homonym of "week days."

Triple Crown

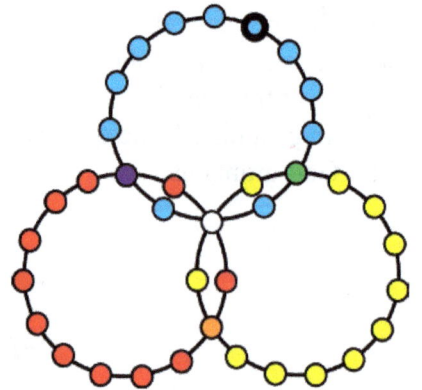

God's Blue Throne

Evermore and more, God grants us rest
From gleaning, 'mid the dust and broken clay,
The crumbs of daily crust which may, at best,
Suppress the pangs of hunger for the day.
Creation's last blue day, when we have done
The work that God created us to do
Reintegrates the broken parts to One
Eternal, unifying sparks anew.
O holy day beyond the mortal ken!
O day we struggle all our days to reach!
O day when we may sigh a last amen,
Restore at last the long neglected breach.[1]
No more to live in yearning I beseech,
Grandiloquent, creating with just speech.

---

[1] See Isaiah 58:12. "Ancient ruins will be rebuilt through you, and you will restore generations-old foundations; and they will call you 'repairer of the breach' and 'restorer of paths for habitation.'"

Triple Crown

Oh let us be united, arms outreach,
Hear songs of love, and poetry recite—
Zither, myrrh, red wine—ev'ry delight
Evoked by love. The waves caress the beach,
As paradise regained swells into reach.
"**L**et there be light," He said, and there was light...
Only once, this dark, this moonless night
The barren walls reverberate a screech—
So cold a night, and none to warm my bed.
So long a night, I scarce recall the days
Of cedar paneled chambers and the vow.
Repeat it now exactly as you said—
Eternally, forever and always!
Delay no moment longer. Take me now!

Oh Zealots So Red

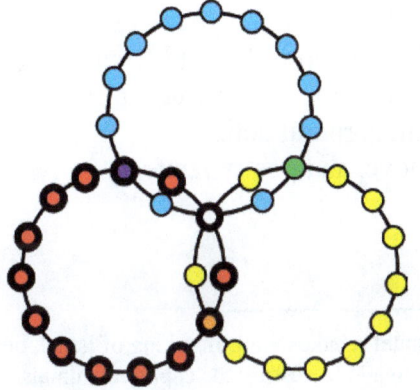

Triple Crown

"Oh let us be united, arms outreach!"
You greet me *thus*? Your greeting only mocks
Your broken state, resounds the wretched bleats
Of pilfered herds forbidden and the flocks [1]
Of reddled rams [2] consigned to death. See there
Your enemy in chains. [3] And yet, this day will bring
For *you* a broken link, [4] for *him* an heir, [5]
Nor spare my robe, [6] your kingdom, or that king.
Oh Saul, my Saul, if only you had been
More than a donkey-chaser in your eyes, [7]
You might have lived in full what life can mean.
Now go—and live a life you must despise:
Go wallow in all corporal delight,
Hear songs of love, and poetry recite.

---

[1] The prophet Samuel rebukes Saul, first king of Israel, because Saul had disobeyed the command to destroy the captured animals. See I Samuel 15:14. "Samuel said, 'And what is this sound of the sheep in my ears and the sound of the cattle that I hear?'"

[2] Reddle (sometimes called ruddle) is a powder made of red ochre. It is used to mark sheep. Cf. the extensive use of reddle in Thomas Hardy's *Return of the Native*.

[3] See I Samuel 15:32. "Samuel then said, 'Bring me Agag, king of Amalek.' Agag went to him in chains…"

[4] See I Samuel 15:23. "…Because you have rejected the word of the Lord, He has rejected you as king!'"

[5] During the time between his capture and execution, Agag sired a son. See Talmud Bavli *Megillah* 13a. "…for Saul did not kill Agag, from whom descended Haman, who oppresses the Jews." See also Esther 3:1. "After these things King Ahasuerus promoted Haman…the Agagite…"

[6] See I Samuel 15:27. "Samuel then turned away to leave, but [Saul] grabbed the hem of his tunic, and it tore."

[7] See I Samuel 15:17. "Samuel said, '…though you may be small in your own eyes…'" See also I Samuel 9:3. "…the donkeys of Kish, Saul's father, were lost, and Kish said to Saul his son, '…search for the donkeys.'"

Oh Zealots So Red

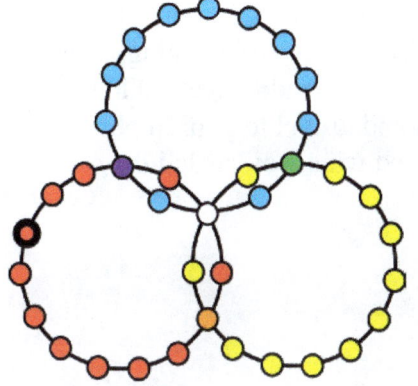

Triple Crown

Hear songs of love, and poetry recite—[1]
And still you'll not escape your rival's hand;
That son of Jesse[2] will not cease to fight
Until he seize your crown, your throne, your land.[3]
And tell me, now, where is your sword, your bow,
Your robe which shows your place above the ranks?[4]
Not traded for a death blow from the foe—
Much worse: you swapped them for a shepherd's thanks.
Ungodly gift,[5] a man who pulls down shame
On all our tribe—my son! Oh what a fall
Is yours! You could have been a king, a name
To long endure. You could have had it all:
Kings to crawl and grovel to your might,
Zither, myrrh, red wine—ev'ry delight.

---

[1] Saul addresses his son Jonathan.
[2] David, who would become the second king of Israel, was a son of Jesse.
[3] See I Samuel 20:30-31. "Saul's anger flared up at Jonathan, and he said to him, 'Son of a pervertedly rebellious woman! Do I not know that you choose the son of Jesse, to your own shame and the shame of your mother's nakedness? For all the days that the son of Jesse is alive on earth, you and your kingdom will not be established!...'"
[4] See I Samuel 18:4. "And Jonathan took off the robe he was wearing and gave it to David; also his battle garments, down to his sword, his bow, and his belt."
[5] The name Jonathan means "God has given."

Oh Zealots So Red

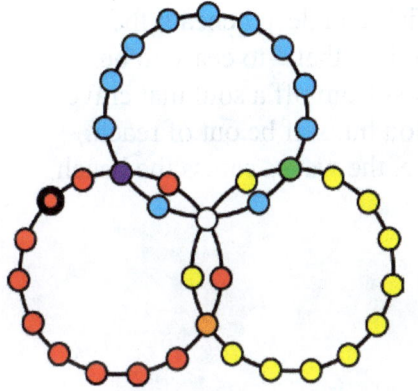

Triple Crown

Zither, myrrh, red wine, ev'ry delight
Betray me too, refuse to satisfy,
Assault my hearing, smell, my taste and sight,[1]
As you, in murmurs, plot to nullify
My battered throne. You crave to do me wrong.
Even village girls with dusty feet
Conspire to mock my conquests with their song,[2]
Emasculate my triumph as defeat.
The blood of my slain thousands flows to sea
To feed their fish-god deep beneath the waves.[3]
How fine an ending that—to cease to be,
To wash the dust from off a soul that craves
No more, of God himself be out of reach.
Evoked by love, the waves caress the beach.

---

[1] In his melancholy, Saul addresses his court. See I Samuel 16:14. "The spirit of the Lord departed from Saul, and he was tormented by a spirit of melancholy from the Lord."

[2] See I Samuel 18:7. "The rejoicing women called out, and said, 'Saul has slain his thousands, and David his tens of thousands.'"

[3] The Philistines worshipped a fish-god named Dagon. See I Samuel 5:1-5, and Rashi *loc.cit.* "…The Philistines took the Ark of God and brought it to the House of Dagon, placing it next to Dagon…"

Oh Zealots So Red

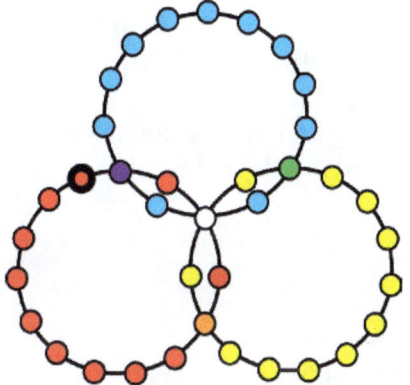

Triple Crown

Evoked by love, the waves caress the beach,[1]
Erasing from the sand all mortal stain
Of struggle and the bleedings that will reach
It, washed in time by river and by rain.
And that will be our end, to perish here
Among these purple irises in bloom,[2]
With blood-stained grass to serve us as a bier,
And flowers crushed to be our only tomb.[3]
And I shall yield my kingdom and my crown—
Yes, I who lost them for a tattered hem—[4]
And like these iris petals lay me down
For all to pluck, impaled upon a stem,[5]
As thirsty swords our waning life-force leech,
As paradise regained swells into reach.

---

[1] Saul addresses his armor-bearer.
[2] Mount Gilboa, where Saul died, is the home of a purple iris called the Gilboa Iris.
[3] Only Saul's bones, not his whole body, were buried. See I Samuel 31:8-13. "…when the Philistines came to plunder the corpses, they found Saul and his three sons, fallen on Mount Gilboa. They severed his head …and hung up his remains upon the wall of Beth-shan…The daring men [of Jabesh-gilead] arose and went throughout the night, and took the remains of Saul and his sons from the wall of Beth-shan, and came back to Jabesh. They burned them there. They then took their bones and buried them under the tamarisk tree in Jabesh…"
[4] See I Samuel 15:27-28. "Samuel then turned away to leave, but [Saul] grabbed the hem of his tunic, and it tore. Samuel said to him, 'The Lord has torn the kingship of Israel from upon you this day, and has given it to your fellow who is better than you.'"
[5] See I Samuel 31:4. "Saul said to his armor-bearer, 'Draw your sword and stab me with it, lest these uncircumcised people come and stab me and make sport of me.' But his armor-bearer did not consent, for he was very frightened, so Saul took the sword himself and fell upon it."

Oh Zealots So Red

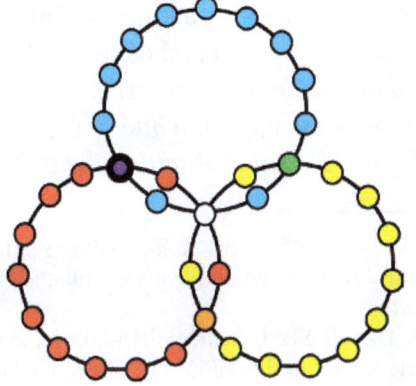

Triple Crown

As paradise regained swells into reach, [1]
He rouses horded treasure of my scent.
The seed that lies within a ruby peach,
So was my hero husband in my tent.
But now you hike your tunic,[2] raise your leg
Like mongrel dogs that piss against a wall.[3]
My daddy earned respect you cannot beg,
Nor ever did he stoop to be so small.[4]
You were not fit to even touch his hem.
How dare you snip his cloak[5]—a king like him!
Your beddings, cold, deny you and condemn.[6]
He was the bridegroom in my chamber dim,
And I the virgin princess clad in white.
"Let there be light," He said. And there was light.

---

[1] Michal was the daughter of Saul whom Saul had given to David as a wife after David heroically slew the Philistine giant Goliath. Her thoughts are indicated by italics.

[2] Michal addresses David. See II Samuel 6:16-20. "And it happened as the Ark of the Lord arrived at the City of David, that Michal daughter of Saul peered out the window and saw king David leaping and dancing before the Lord, and she became contemptuous of him in her heart…and said, 'How honored was the king of Israel today, who was exposed today in the presence of his servants' maidservants, as one of the boors would be exposed!'"

[3] See I Samuel 25:22. The phrase משתין בקיר is sometimes translated as "a dog," but literally means one who urinates against a wall.

[4] Saul was unusually tall. See I Samuel 9:2. "[Kish] had a son named Saul who was exceptional and good-looking; no one in Israel was more handsome than he. From his shoulders up, he was taller than any of the people."

[5] See I Samuel 24:4-5. "…there was a cave there, which Saul entered to relieve himself. David and his men were sitting at the far end of the cave…So David arose and stealthily cut off a corner of Saul's robe."

[6] See I Kings 1:1. "King David was old, advanced in years. They covered him with garments, but he did not become warm." See also Talmud Bavli *Berachos* 62b: "Whoever dishonors clothing will in the end not have use of them."

Oh Zealots So Red

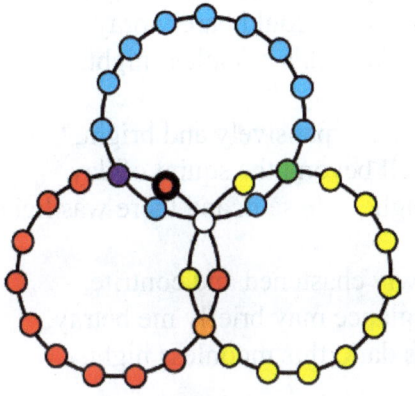

47

Triple Crown

"Let there be light," He said, and there was light,[1]
But you enticed me and I went astray[2]
Only once, this dark, this moonless night.

You snuffed my lamp; your shadow veiled my sight,
And so unseen I could not see the way
"Let there be light," He said, and there was light.

Your ribbons wrapped about me, lacing tight;[3]
Into the depths I sank, could barely pray
Only once, this dark, this moonless night.

God answered me expansively and bright,[4]
In brilliance well beyond the squint of day.
"Let there be light," He said, and there was light.

Reflecting, newly chastened and contrite,
My backward glance may briefly me betray,
Only once, this dark, this moonless night.

Though I, in twilight, penances recite,[5]
The image of that night does not decay:
"Let there be light," He said, and there was light
Only once, this dark, this moonless night.

---

[1] David addresses Bathsheba. Bathsheba was the wife of Uriah, an officer in David's army. David impregnated Bathsheba, and later arranged for Uriah to be sent to the battlefront, where he would be killed.
[2] See II Samuel 11:1-5. "…She came to him and he lay with her…"
[3] See Jonah 2:6-7. "Waters encompassed me to the soul, the deep whirled around me; reeds were tangled about my head. I descended to the bases of the mountains; the earth—its bars were closed against me forever."
[4] See Psalms 118:5. "From the straits did I call upon God; God answered me with expansiveness."
[5] See Psalms 51:5. "For I recognize my transgressions, and my sin is before me always."

Oh Zealots So Red

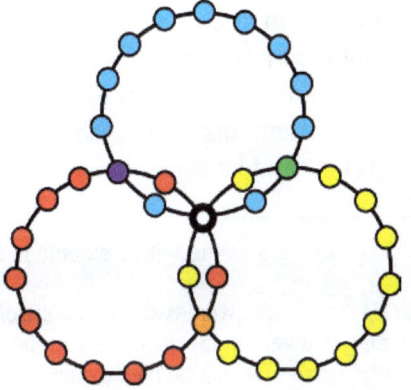

Triple Crown

Only once, this dark, this moonless night[1]
He reached out, quite by habit—she was gone,
Who'd shared his bread, his cup, his bed.[2] Delight
Itself the thief had grabbed. What's to be done
To such a one, my king—how do you hold?
Yes, justice will proceed just as you plan;
He merits death, must compensate fourfold.[3]
Now one more thing, my king: *You* are that man![4]
Anointed one of God, you have forsaken
God, and pampered evil in your heart.
Now from your sundered house will four be taken,[5]
The blood-stained dripping sword will not depart.[6]
When justice to the battlements will reach,
The barren walls reverberate a screech.

---

[1] The prophet Nathan challenges David with a parable in the form of a legal case.

[2] See II Samuel 12:1-4. "...There were two men in one city; one rich and one poor. The rich man had very many sheep and cattle, but the poor man had nothing except one small ewe that he had acquired. He raised it and it grew up together with him and his children. It ate from his bread and drank from his cup and lay in his bosom; it became like a daughter to him...The rich man took the poor man's ewe..."

[3] See II Samuel 12:5-6. "David was very indignant about this man, and he said to Nathan, 'As the Lord lives, any man who does this deserves to die! And he must pay fourfold for the ewe, because he did this deed and because he had no pity!'" See also Exodus 21:37. "If a man shall steal an ox, or a sheep or goat, and slaughter it or sell it, he shall pay five cattle in place of the ox, and four sheep in place of the sheep."

[4] See II Samuel 12:7. "Nathan then said to David, 'You are that man!'"

[5] See Talmud Bavli *Yoma* 12b. In fact, four were indeed taken from among David's offsprings: Bathsheba's first-born child, who died in infancy (II Samuel 2:18); Tamar, who was raped (II Samuel 13:14); Amnon, who was murdered in revenge by his half-brother (II Samuel 13:29); and Absalom, who died in a war of rebellion against his father (II Samuel 18:14-15).

[6] See II Samuel 12:10. "And now, the sword shall not cease from your house forever, because you have scorned Me and have taken the wife of Uriah the Hittite to be a wife unto you."

Oh Zealots So Red

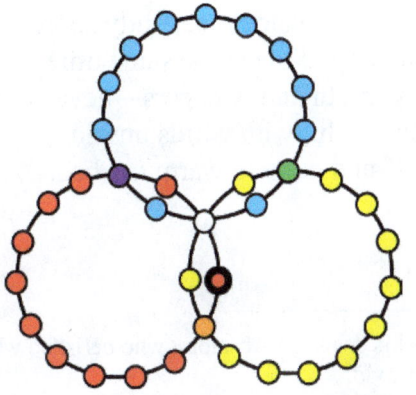

Triple Crown

The barren walls reverberate a screech—[1]
My son, my son, O Absalom, my son![2]
But daddy's lullabies will no more reach
My son, my son, O Absalom, my son!
No more, my son, I'll peel the prickly pear[3]
For you, no more embrace you while my fingers
Plow love furrows through your crown of hair.[4]
Gone is hope, my son,[5] though yearning lingers.
Gone too those chilly nights when you would climb
Into my bed, and curl beside me, gently snore,
And warm yourself and me at the same time.
Such nights of warmth and whispers—nevermore!
Reverberant, this night, with words unsaid;
So cold a night—and none to warm my bed.

---

[1] David addresses his dead son Absalom, who perished while leading a rebellion against David.
[2] See II Samuel 19:1-5. "The king trembled. He ascended to the upper chamber of the gateway and wept; and thus he said as he went: 'My son, Absalom! My son, my son, Absalom! If only I could have died in your place! Absalom, my son, my son!'...The king wrapped his face, and the king cried out in a loud voice, 'My son, Absalom! Absalom, my son, my son!'"
[3] In Israel, the prickly pear is known as the *sabra*. Native-born Israelis have adopted the name for themselves, since the fruit is prickly on the outside, but sweet on the inside. The sweet pulp of the fruit is orange in color.
[4] Absalom had remarkably abundant hair. See II Samuel 14:26. "When [Absalom] would have his head barbered—at the end of every year he would have his hair barbered, because it became heavy upon him and he had it barbered—the hair of his head weighed two hundred shekels by the king's weight."
[5] According to Talmud Bavli *Sotah* 10b, David uttered the word(s) "my son" eight times—seven times to raise Absalom from the seven chambers of Gehinnom (the underworld), and one more time to elevate him to the World to Come.

Oh Zealots So Red

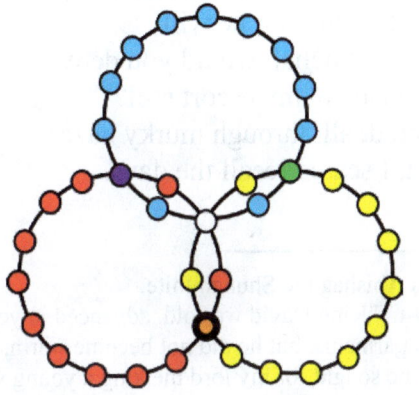

Triple Crown

So cold a night, and none to warm my bed[1]
But you, a youthful stranger hired to spend
The night, to hear my stories dear and dread,
And nod and wonder too when will it end.[2]
I killed a giant once,[3] six cubits high
Or more,[4] cut off his bloody head and raised
It by the hair.[5] But surely that's not why—
O Absalom! God's anger also blazed
Against the baby.[6] Better *I* should die.
O Absalom! I'll go to him; he will
Not come to me.[7] Michal, would you deny
A king? Oh, Jonathan, my escort still?[8]
I see you gathered, all, through murky haze.
So long a night, I scarce recall the days.

---

[1] David addresses Abishag the Shunammite.
[2] See I Kings 1:1-4. "King David was old, advanced in years. They covered him with garments, but he did not become warm. His servants said to him, 'Let there be sought for my lord the king a young virgin, who will stand before the king and be his attendant; she will lie in your bosom and it will be warm for my lord the king...They found Abishag the Shunammite and brought her to the king. The girl was exceedingly beautiful, and she became the king's attendant and she served him, but the king was not intimate with her."
[3] As he lies dying, David's mind drifts into terminal hallucinations.
[4] See I Samuel 17:4. "A champion went forth from the Philistine camps, whose name was Goliath of Gath; his height was six cubits and one span."
[5] See I Samuel 17:54. "David took the head of the Philistine, and [eventually] brought it to Jerusalem..."
[6] See II Samuel 12:18. "It happened on the seventh day that [Bathsheba's newborn] child died..."
[7] See II Samuel 12:23. "...[David said] 'Can I bring him back again? I will be going to him, but he will not return to me.'"
[8] Jonathan escorted David as he fled from Saul. See I Samuel 20:42. "Jonathan said to David, 'Go to peace. What the two of us have sworn in the name of the Lord—saying the Lord shall be [a witness] between me and you, and between my offspring and your offspring—shall be forever!'"

Oh Zealots So Red

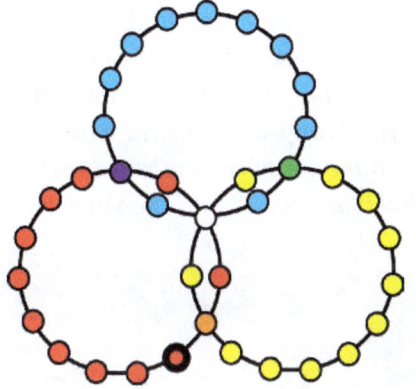

Triple Crown

So long a night, I scarce recall the days[1]
Before ambition seized my widowed heart.
Yes, open, lord, my lips; I'll tell your praise.[2]
A girl of seven years can play this part.[3]
Remember, husband-king, the vow you made
Before we wed: "Your son will reign," you said,[4]
"When, with my fathers, I at last am laid
Forever in my shroud and cedar bed."
Now may you live forever, O my lord.
Now crown my son and seat him on your chair,
Your red-eyed wife and nation have implored.
While still your life hangs by its brittle hair,[5]
Let only these two thoughts your mind allow:
Of cedar paneled chambers,[6] *and the vow.*

---

[1] Bathsheba was the wife of David, and mother of Solomon. Here Bathsheba addresses David. Her inner thoughts are in italics.
[2] Bathsheba quotes Psalm 51:15, but with a very different meaning from that in the text.
[3] The name Bathsheba means "seven-year-old girl" in Hebrew.
[4] See I Kings 1:17. "[Bathsheba] said to [David], 'My lord, you swore to your maidservant by the Lord your God: only Solomon, your son, will reign after me, and he will sit on my throne.'"
[5] Brittle hair, cold intolerance and mental clouding are symptoms of end-stage hypothyroidism, a possible cause of David's death.
[6] In the Iron Age, some royalty in the Levant were buried in cedar coffins.

Oh Zealots So Red

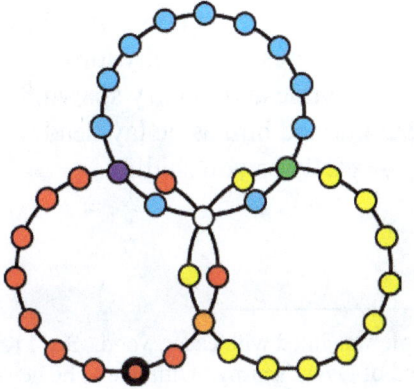

Triple Crown

Of cedar paneled chambers,[1] and the vow
That Joab[2] swore, and how your foe did cling
In vain to our most holy shrine,[3] I'll now
Relate, my lord—and may your servant bring
A smile of pleasure to your face.[4] He swore
He'd never leave that place—and it was so.
Defile the altar with his very gore—
That was his plan—and with that same blood flow
To stain your name. He mocked you, said the sword
Devours this way and that,[5] and now, withdrawn
From him, his curse inures to you, my lord:
Impure and leprous, lame and hungry spawn.[6]
I struck—and summoned him as he lay dead,
"Repeat it *now*—exactly as you said!"

---

[1] Solomon's Temple was lined with cedar wood. See I Kings 6:15.

[2] Joab was the head of David's army. Ultimately, he betrayed David by supporting an attempted *coup d'état*. On the brink of his death, David told Solomon to have Joab killed. Solomon sent his servant Benaiah to carry out the killing

[3] Seeking sanctuary, Joab fled to the holy tabernacle. See I Kings 2:28. "…Joab fled to the Tent of the Lord and took hold of the horns of the Altar."

[4] Benaiah addresses Solomon.

[5] Years earlier, David had secretly instructed Joab to expose Uriah to the brunt of the enemy forces. Joab did so. Afterward, David tried to placate Joab with the very words Joab now repeats here. See II Samuel 11:25. "David then told the messenger, 'Say thus to Joab: Do not let this matter be deemed evil in your eyes, for the sword consumes one way or another…'"

[6] Earlier, against David's wishes, Joab had killed Abner, a leader of Saul's military forces, shortly after Abner had switched sides to support David. David therefore cursed Joab concerning his progeny. See II Samuel 3:29. "…[David said] may there never cease from Joab's house contaminated men, lepers, those who lean on crutches, who fall by the sword, and who lack food." So it was. See Talmud Bavli *Sanhedrin* 48b for details.

Oh Zealots So Red

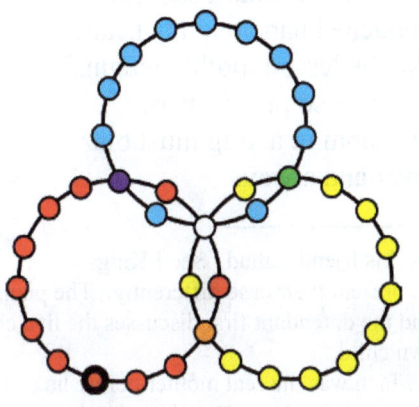

Triple Crown

"Repeat it now exactly as you said."[1]
I told them that for you, Zabud, not me.
Which mother had the live son, which the dead,
Was clear to me when each had made her plea.[2]
But how to get my court to know that fact?[3]
I ordered that the boy be cut in two,
And both of them were certain to react
Exactly as they did for all to view.[4]
The wisdom of a king is what I sought,[5]
To know the reddened hand and icy heart,
And not forsake the lesson mother taught.[6]
A king, in wisdom, also plays a part.
Such burning wisdom in a king must blaze
Eternally, forever and always.

---

[1] Solomon address his friend Zabud. See I Kings 4:5.
[2] The two women present their case differently. The plaintiff first discusses the dead child, and the defendant first discusses the live child. Each is first describing her own child.
[3] Solomon knew which was the real mother before he ordered that a sword be brought to cut the child in half. But if he simply made a ruling, the court might think that the decision was arbitrary or incorrect.
[4] Solomon recognized that the two women were living together without a man because they were mother- and daughter-in-law, both of whose husbands had recently died. The daughter-in-law (the plaintiff) had a motive to lie, because then she would appear to be relieved of having to wait until the boy were 13 years old to relieve her of the duty of levirate marriage (*yibum*). All the more so, she had a motive to see the child killed by the king, because then in actuality, not merely appearance, she would be released from a levirate marriage. It is ordinary insight to recognize that a woman who is willing to have the baby killed is not the real mother. But Solomon knew that the false claimant would not simply say, "See! She says give the baby to me. She is willing to kidnap, but not to murder!" His wisdom lay in his knowing that she would agree to having the baby killed, not merely in recognizing that her saying so identified her as the false claimant.
[5] See I Kings 3:5-9.
[6] See Proverbs 1:8.

Oh Zealots So Red

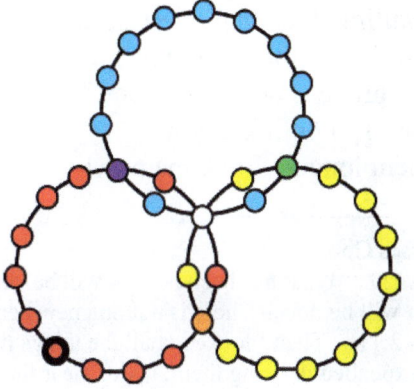

Triple Crown

Eternally, forever, and always—[1]
And no thing new is seen beneath the sun.
The endless shuffling march of nights and days:
What was, will be; what will be has been done.[2]
You gave me wisdom, Lord, as I had sought,
And made me rich in flocks and oil and grain.
To what avail? For all of this is naught,
Nor ever will be more, for all is vain.[3]
The wise man and the fool have the same end.[4]
All laughter, wailing, bleeding likewise cease.
What misers horde, another man will spend,[5]
And even in the grave is doubtful peace.[6]
Before your pow'r to nullify I bow.[7]
Delay no moment longer. Take me now!

---

[1] Solomon addresses God.
[2] See Ecclesiastes 1:9. "What has been is what will be, and whatever has been done is what will be done. There is nothing new beneath the sun."
[3] See Ecclesiastes 2:11. "Then I looked at all the things that I had done and the energy I had expended in doing them; it was clear that it was all futile and a vexation of the spirit—and there is no real profit under the sun." Also See *Shir Ha-shirim Rabba* 1:10. "Rabbi Yonatan said that [Solomon] wrote Song of Songs first, then Proverbs, and then Ecclesiastes. He brought a proof from the way of the world: when a man is young he sings love songs, in middle-age he tells parables, and in old age he speaks of the vanities of the world."
[4] See Ecclesiastes 2:14. "The wise man has his eyes in his head, whereas a fool walks in darkness. But I also realized that the same fate awaits them all."
[5] See Ecclesiastes 6:2. "God may give a man riches, wealth, and honor, so that he lack nothing that the heart could desire, yet God does not give him the power to enjoy it; instead, a stranger will enjoy it."
[6] See Ecclesiastes 3:19-21. "…Man has no superiority over beast, for all is futile. All go to the same place; all originate from dust and all return to dust. Who perceives that the spirit of man is the one that ascends on high, while the spirit of the beast is the one that descends down into the earth?"
[7] See Ecclesiastes 4:2. "So I consider more fortunate the dead who have already died than the living who are still alive…"

Oh Zealots So Red

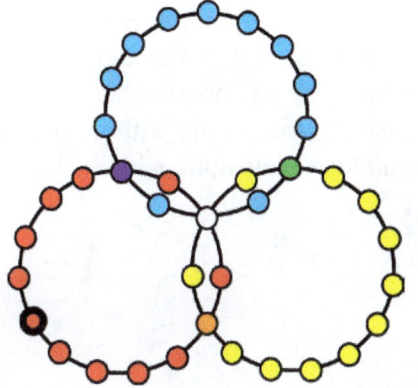

Triple Crown

Delay no moment longer. Take me now
To see the men at arms who guard the land…[1]
You soldiers know what threats we face, and how
To fight. Now shout: United! Arms in hand!
Our enemies would cut our land in two,[2]
Would spill our babies' blood, and their war cry
Would rend the air. But this they shall not do!
Let us shout: United! Arms held high!
United shall we pacify our land
From Dan unto Beersheba,[3] and our reach
Extend from our great river to the strand
Where pummel salty waves upon the beach.[4]
One God! One land! One people without breach,
Oh let us be! United! Arms outreach!

---

[1] Solomon addresses his army.
[2] After his death, Solomon's kingdom was divided into rival monarchies.
[3] See I Kings 5:5. "Judah and Israel dwelt in security, each man under his grapevine and under his fig tree, from Dan unto Beersheba, all the days of Solomon."
[4] See Joshua 1:3-4. "Every place upon which the sole of your foot will tread I have given to you, as I spoke to Moses. From the desert and this Lebanon until the great river, the Euphrates River, all the land of the Hittites until the Great Sea toward the setting of the sun will be your boundary."

Oh Zealots So Red

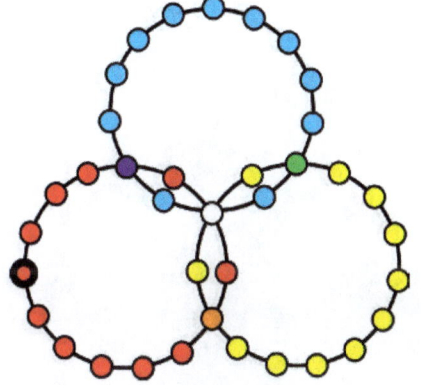

Triple Crown

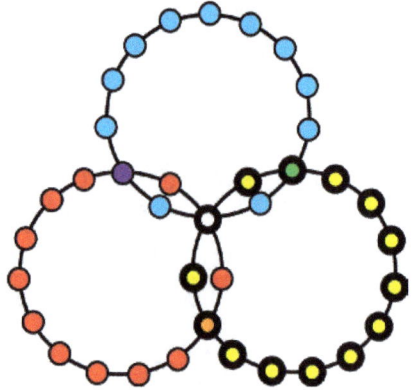

Dust—All's Yellow

Desire itself no longer within reach,
Unstinting and severe, the hands that smite—
Such justice, and its judge, do I indict.
The barren walls reverberate a screech
As muzzy-mumble sages nod and teach
"**L**et there be light," He said, and there was light.
Like scattered stars abandoned to the night,
Safeguard them nigh—and me within your reach
You may destroy, completely extirpate.
Erase the yellowed parchment, start anew.
Lament some other human tragedy,
Lest man believe that he is thrall to fate.
One is ever one and never two,
When time and separation cease to be.

Triple Crown

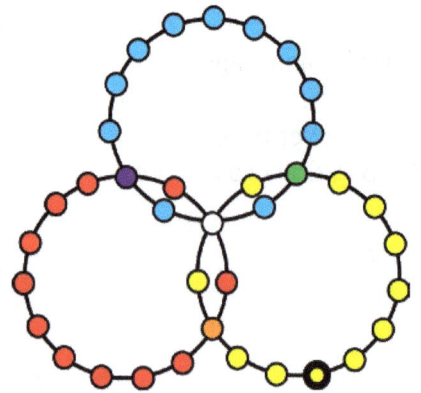

Dust—All's Yellow

Desire itself no longer within reach,[1]
I still recall when I could feel its grip,
When any wanted thing, mere whispered speech
Would place into my hand, nor would it slip
From out my grasp.[2] And more: I was content!
I did not know the maggot gnaw of greed,
But knew the joy of gold and time well spent.
I knew the gratitude of those in need
Of generosity with wealth to match.[3]
Now gone, all gone! All felled within an hour!
The forces of misfortune thus could snatch
My slow accreted honor, wealth, and pow'r.
The brightness of my day enshrouds my night.
Unstinting and severe, the hands that smite.

---

[1] The inability to anticipate pleasure is a hallmark of depression.
[2] See Job 1:1-3. "There was a man in the land of Uz whose name was Job; that man was wholesome and upright, he feared God and shunned evil. Seven sons and three daughters were born to him. His possessions consisted of seven thousand sheep and goats, three thousand camels, five hundred pairs of cattle, five hundred she-donkeys, and very many enterprises. That man was the wealthiest man of all the people in the East."
[3] See Job 29:12-16. "For I would rescue a pauper from his wailing, and an orphan who had no one to help him. The blessings of the forlorn would be upon me, and I would bring joyous song to a widow's heart. I donned righteousness, and it suited me; my justice was like a cloak and a headdress. I was eyes to the blind, and feet to the lame; I was a father to the destitute; if I was ignorant of their grievance I would investigate."

Triple Crown

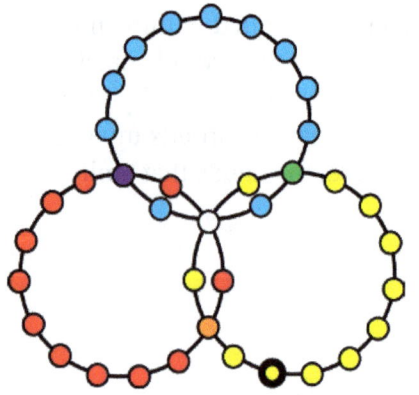

Dust—All's Yellow

Unstinting and severe, the hands that smite,
That strangle the newborn with its own cord,
That justify injustice with just might:
I summon now to justice nature's lord.[1]
I witness—I alone am left to tell—
That ten were wrenched like fingers from my hands
And crushed together, buried where they fell,
Entombed beneath the stones and yellow sands.[2]
No daughter's corpse was left me to inter,
Nor son to bury me. Ten children—dead!
Then came my friends to comfort, to confer
Their peace on me.[3] "God's ways are just" they said,
"He rules the world with justice and with might."
Such justice, and its judge, do I indict.

---

[1] See Job 10:1-7. "I speak out in the bitterness of my soul. I say to God: Do not condemn me. Tell me why You contend with me. Does it befit You to plunder, that You despise the labor of Your hands, but glow upon the schemes of the wicked? Do You have eyes of flesh? Do You see as a man sees? Are Your days like a person's days, are Your years like a man's days, that You search out my iniquity and seek my transgression? You know that I will not be found guilty, yet none can save from Your hand."

[2] See Job 1:18-19. "This one was still speaking, when another one came and said, 'Your sons and your daughters were eating and drinking wine in the home of their eldest brother, when behold, a great wind came from across the desert. It struck the four corners of the house, it collapsed upon the youths and killed them. Only I, by myself, escaped to tell you!'"

[3] See Job 2:11-14. "Job's three friends heard about this total calamity that had befallen him, and each one of them came from his place: Eliphaz the Temanite, Bildad the Shuhite, and Zophar the Naamathite. They gathered together to go and mourn with him and comfort him. They raised their eyes from a distance, but did not recognize him. They raised their voices and wept, each man rent his coat, and they threw dust over their heads toward heaven. They sat with him on the ground for a period of seven days and seven nights. No one said a word to him, for they saw that his pain was very great. After that, Job opened his mouth and cursed his day."

Triple Crown

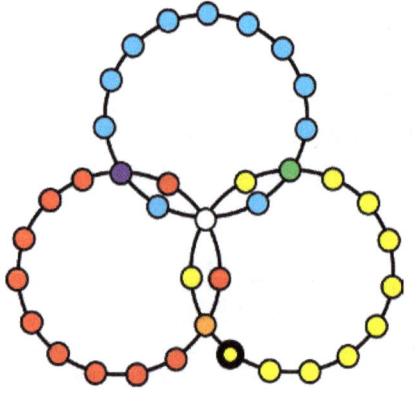

Dust—All's Yellow

Such justice, and its judge, do I indict:
Omnipotent, inscrutable, and far
From reason to or reason not to smite
The flesh in which we live or which we are.[1]
My flesh, a charnel feast where flies may spawn,
Precedes me into death. I sit in dust,
Ooze life, and with a greasy ostracon[2]
Scrape from my wounds repugnant honey crust.[3]
O flesh so fair, so faithless to your form,
So foul and fetid now, a wounded field,
Repulsive to all life except the worm!
And what avail my prayers? He is concealed.[4]
No answer comes whence imprecations reach.
The barren walls reverberate a screech.

---

[1] Job questions whether there is more to man than his body.

[2] An ostracon is synonymous with a potsherd. Ostraca were used in Greek society as a tool for ostracizing members from society. See Job 2:8. "The Satan departed from the presence of the Lord, and afflicted Job with severe boils, from the soles of his feet to the top of his head. He took a potsherd to scratch himself with, and he sat amid the ashes."

[3] Many skin diseases, and impetigo in particular, are characterized by honey-colored scabs formed from dried serum.

[4] See Job 3:19-22. "Why does He give light to the sufferer, and life to those bitter of soul; to those who crave death but it is not there, who seek it more eagerly than hidden treasure; to those who, exulting as if at a joyous occasion, rejoice when they find the grave; to the man whose deeds are concealed, before whom God has raised a barrier?"

Triple Crown

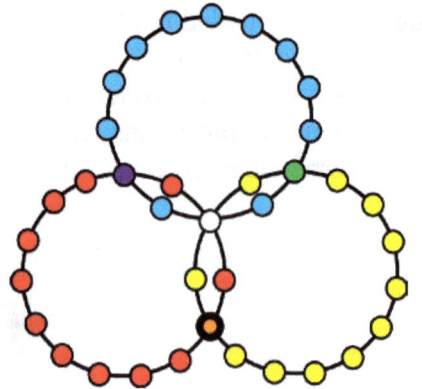

Dust—All's Yellow

The barren walls reverberate a screech
Of frantic ululation, words aflame.
The barren mother,[1] desp'rate, claws to reach
For cause, for purpose, meaning—or for blame.
"Disease and dispossession, graceless death
Do not befall the sinless. While I live,"
She says, "I hate you, 'til my final breath,
Excoriate your name, and not forgive.
Curse God and die."[2] She never speaks again.
We eat our lentils silently and cold,[3]
And silently and cold she knows my pain
Is more than she can bear, and she has told
The bold and dread conclusion I must reach,
As muzzy-mumble sages nod and teach.

---

[1] Job's wife, too, is now childless.
[2] See Job 2:9. "His wife said to him, 'Do you still maintain your wholesomeness? Blaspheme God and die!'"
[3] The lentils of the Middle East are orange in color. Lentils are a traditional and symbolic meal of mourning. Like a mourner whose mouth cannot speak his anguish, so the lentil has no "mouth" [indentation]. Just as death in time rolls over all of mankind, so the lentil is shaped like a wheel.

Triple Crown

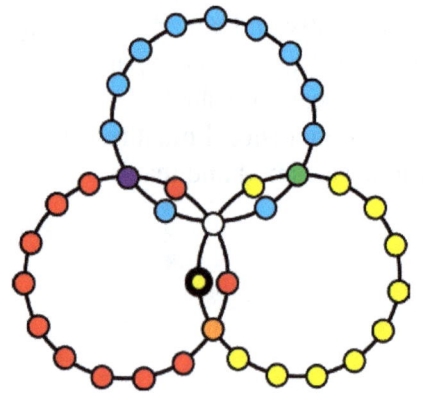

Dust—All's Yellow

As muzzy-mumble sages nod and teach
Of worlds they've never seen, they promise there
Is found the world of truth. And as they preach,
I scrape my skin in loathing and despair.
Here is the truth: the yellow scum I scrape
From stinking flesh. Here is the truth: the loss
Of all I was, the truth none can escape,
Reality revealed in all its dross.
The death of hope illuminates the world,
Allows no further loss, no more deceit,
No blessings, curses, imprecations hurled,
No more illusions ceaseless to repeat.
The truth is revelation blinding bright.
"Let there be light," He said, and there was light.

Triple Crown

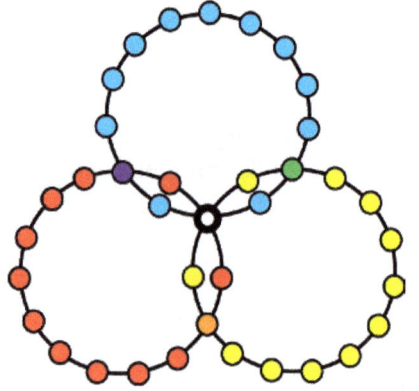

Dust—All's Yellow

"Let there be light," He said, and there was light,
So long ago and now so far away,
Like scattered stars abandoned to the night.

The world, which once we thought could hold delight,
A wasteland[1] now, it mocks the wasted day
"Let there be light," He said, and there was light.

And we too have been banished from His sight,
Invisible, to blindly feel our way,
Like scattered stars abandoned to the night.

Nor shall we know redemption from our plight,
Nor does this hoary fact our grief allay:
"Let there be light," He said, and there was light.

Like dust indifferent wind blows from a height,
We float unseen, and slowly drift away,
Like scattered stars abandoned to the night.

How grand was the creation—and how slight
The part, if any, we are called to play.
"Let there be light," He said, and there was light,
Like scattered stars abandoned to the night.

---

[1] An *homage* to "The Waste Land" by T.S. Eliot:
"…What are the roots that clutch, what branches grow
Out of this stony rubbish? Son of man,
You cannot say, or guess, for you know only
A heap of broken images, where the sun beats,
And the dead tree gives no shelter, the cricket no relief,
And the dry stone no sound of water…"

Triple Crown

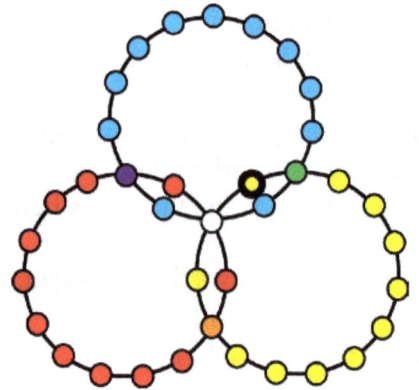

Dust—All's Yellow

Like scattered stars abandoned to the night,
Too feeble the great darkness to adorn,
Now come my friends to loom athwart my light,
To triply crown my sorrow with their scorn.
"The world was not created," says the first,[1]
"To be surrendered, sundered in the maw
Of chaos. Rather, from the primal burst
Continues on its course and by its law.
The close of day, the yellow autumn's end,
The crumbling of a wall, a kingdom's fall,
Our shabby motley fabric and its rend
Convince the fool that chaos governs all.
The wise will see this, bow in awe, beseech,
'Safeguard them nigh, and me, within your reach.'"

---

[1] See Job 4-5. Job's first comforter, Eliphaz, argues that the world is justly run according to divinely established natural laws.

Triple Crown

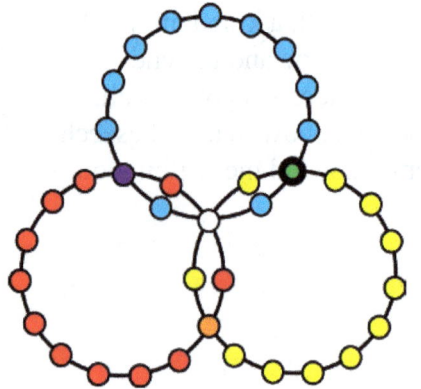

Dust—All's Yellow

Safeguard them nigh, and me, within your reach—
A child's prayer before he goes to bed,
The twice-chewed cud of empty prattle speech
Before his throat is clutched in claws of dread.
Oh, yes, the world has laws by which it's run
In mulish bondage to its master's plan.
But justice! Where is justice? There is none![1]
Condemned to live in vain and die is man,
For he alone has knowledge of his fate,
And will to will the world as it is not.
For every day's tomorrow must he wait,
And every yesterday relive in thought.
And me, O God, whose death will come too late,
You may destroy, completely extirpate.

---

[1] See Job 6-7. Job responds to Eliphaz, saying that while the world may be orderly, it lacks justice.

Triple Crown

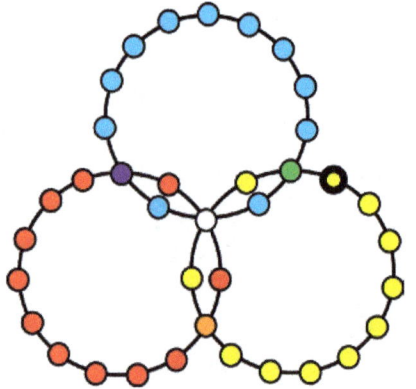

Dust—All's Yellow

"You may destroy, completely extirpate,"
Replies the second friend, "That final spark
Still glowing in your soul, ascribe to fate
The recompense of man, and in your dark
Cascade deny the light.[1] This you may do
Oblivious to truth. The blind deny
The light while staring at the sun—and you
Howl 'Justice!' just as justice you defy.
Yet consequence is plain to see for all,
Unscrolled in time, writ large and fair, condign.
Your scroll, though now a smudged and angry scrawl,
Could be a palimpsest of your design.
Your plaint is common, shameful, and untrue.
Erase the yellowed parchment, start anew."

---

[1] Job's second comforter, Bildad, argues that there is in fact justice in the world, implying that Job may not be as innocent as he claims. See Job 8. "Bildad the Shuhite then spoke up and said: 'How long will you say such things? The words of your mouth are a powerful wind! Would God pervert justice? What the Almighty pervert righteousness? When your sons sinned against Him, He delivered them into the hand of their own transgression...'"

Triple Crown

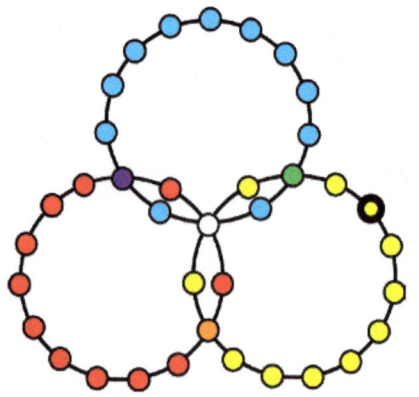

Dust—All's Yellow

Erase the yellowed parchment, start anew—
A foolish hope, a vain and futile goal.
I am the sum of all I've suffered through;
Without my scars I'd be another soul.
No, better I had died before my birth,[1]
Or swaddling cloths had been my tiny shroud—
I'd not complain of justice and its dearth.
Existence, to be honest, is not cowed,
But howls the hated truth though none believe.
Myself alone I know, and you do not,
And to unsullied innocence I cleave
In isolation by injustice wrought.[2]
I cannot, till my justice come to me,
Lament some other human tragedy.

---

[1] See Job 3:10. "Why did I not die from the womb, [not] expire as I came forth from the belly?"
[2] Job replies that there is no justice for *him*.

Triple Crown

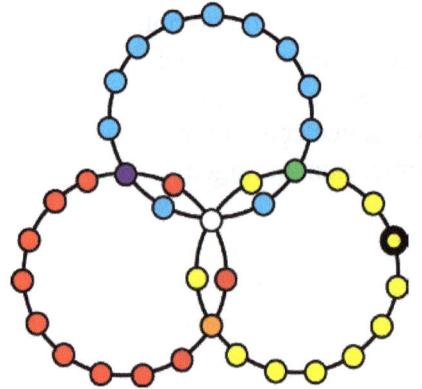

Dust—All's Yellow

"Lament some other human tragedy,"
Replies my final friend. "No more assault
Our ears with self-indulgent threnody
For losses which, in truth, are your own fault.[1]
You did not rail against divine decree
While basking in your health and wealth and name;
Now just conviction makes you disagree.
Vituperate yourself, for you're to blame.
You planted vetch, and now would harvest grape,
Sinned secretly, now innocence declaim.
The honey-crusted oozings that you scrape
Make evident your guilt, if not your shame.
Confess. Repent.[2] No longer desecrate,
Lest man believe that he is thrall to fate."

---

[1] Job's third comforter, Zophar, directly challenges Job's claim of innocence, and tells Job that his misery is a just punishment for his wickedness. See Job 11. "Zophar the Naamathite then spoke up and said: 'Should an effusive speaker not be answered? Is an eloquent orator correct? Your fabrications strike men dumb; you scoff, and no one ridicules you. You say, 'My teaching is pure; I am virtuous in Your eyes.' But if God would speak and open His lips to you, He would relate to you hidden recesses of wisdom, for His sagacity is manifold. Know, then, that God exacts from you *less* than your iniquities!"

[2] Confession precedes repentance. See Proverbs 28:13. "One who conceals his sins will not succeed, but he who confesses and forsakes them will be granted mercy."

Triple Crown

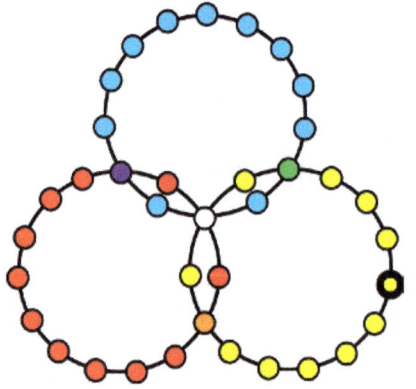

Dust—All's Yellow

Lest man believe that he is thrall to fate.
Or history unfurls without an aim,
I call on God. Appear[1]—and advocate
My claim of innocence. Or if You blame
Me for transgressions, state Your case.[2] Remind me
Of Your storied truth, at last reveal
Your hidden justice, tell me why You grind me
Like a pollen grain beneath Your heel.
You are one, alone, unique in awe;
I am one, alone, unique in woe.
Establish justice, melding truth with law,
Not just in lofty heights, but here below.
Duplicity deny and faith renew.
One is ever one and never two.

---

[1] See Psalms 94:1-2. "O God of vengeance, Lord; O God of vengeance, appear! Arise, O Judge of the earth, render recompense to the haughty."
[2] Job continues to plead his innocence and demands that God respond to his testimony. See Job 13:17-23. "Hear well my words, and let my expression be in Your ears. Behold, I have arranged my argument; I know that I will be vindicated. Who is he that would contend with me? Were I to keep silent now, I would expire. Just do not do these two things to me, and I will not conceal myself from Your presence: Remove Your hand from upon me, and let not fear of You terrify me. Call out and I will answer; or else let me speak, and You respond. How many iniquities and sins have I? Apprise me of my transgression and my sin! Why do you hide Your face and consider me as an enemy unto You?"

Triple Crown

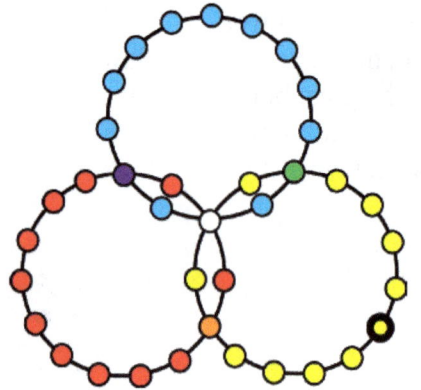

Dust—All's Yellow

"One is ever one and never two."[1]
A prisoner in flesh, <u>you</u> comprehend?
Ex nihilo, a mustard seed;[2] *I grew*
The cosmos end to end to without end.
Who set the thumb to perfectly appose,
To set in place a single errant hair?
Who quickens life within the womb's repose,
Effecting life in water as in air?
Who taught the foot to jerk and pull away
Before the pain, when just pricked by a pin?[3]
Who sets the stars above in their display,
Illuminates the moral sense within?[4]
I was, I am, I shall—eternally,
When time and separation[5] *cease to be.*

---

[1] God answers Job. The Creator is characterized by unity; creation is characterized by duality (such as the wave-particle duality described by quantum mechanics). See Job 38-39. "The Lord responded to Job from out of the whirlwind, and said: 'Who is this who gives murky counsel, with words without knowledge? Gird your loins like a warrior, and I will ask you, and you will inform Me. Where were you when I laid the earth's foundation? Tell, if you know understanding! Who set its dimensions—if you know—or who stretched a surveyor's line over it?...'"

[2] Nachmanides, in *Toras Hashem Temima* writes that God created the world from absolute nothingness. "The thing that was created was a small object that was as small as a mustard seed; this was the heavens and everything in them." This description is similar to that of the standard model Big Bang theory.

[3] When the foot is pricked by a pin, the leg pulls away even before pain is perceived.

[4] Cf. Immanuel Kant, *Critique of Practical Reason*: "Two things fill the mind with ever-increasing wonder and awe, the more often and the more intensely the mind of thought is drawn to them: the starry heavens above me and the moral law within me."

[5] Space-time distinguishes, that is, separates otherwise identical simultaneous events at the same place.

Triple Crown

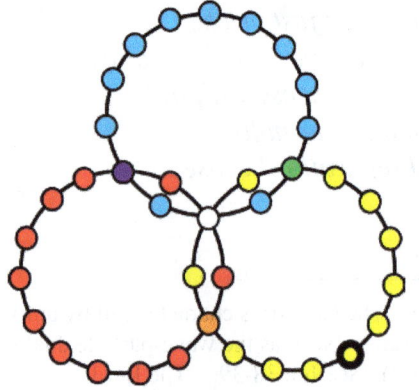

Dust—All's Yellow

When time and separation cease to be
A stranglehold unstinting and severe
Athwart the very breath that breathes in me,
The timeless far is now so very near.
And poverty no longer makes me poor,
And loneliness no longer all alone.
The pain, unchanged, persistent, without cure,
No longer makes me suffer, though I groan.
Omnipotent You are, as I have heard,
But now my eyes have seen You, and your speech
Grandiloquent to me excels Your word.[1]
If in this yellow dust the sun would bleach
My bones, I'm still content, repaired the breach,
Desire itself no longer within reach.[2]

---

[1] See Job 42:5. "I had heard of You through hearsay, but now my eye has beheld You! Therefore, I renounce my words and relent, for I am but dust and ashes."
[2] One who has all he wants cannot desire.

www.ingramcontent.com/pod-product-compliance
Lightning Source LLC
Chambersburg PA
CBHW071158090426
42736CB00012B/2369